THIRST

THIRST

Poems by

Mary Oliver

BEACON PRESS

BOSTON

Beacon Press
Boston, Massachusetts
www.beacon.org

Beacon Press books
are published under the auspices of
the Unitarian Universalist Association of Congregations.

Text design by Dede Cummings/dcdesign

The epigraph on page ix comes from *The Sayings of the Desert Fathers,* Benedicta Ward, SLG, translator. Copyright 1975 by Sister Benedicta. Published by Cistercian Publications Inc.

27 26 25 24   18

ISBN 978-0-8070-6896-0 (hc.)
ISBN 978-0-8070-6897-7 (pbk.)

This book is printed on acid-free paper that meets the uncoated paper ANSI/NISO specifications for permanence as revised in 1992.

Library of Congress Control Number: 2006928745

For
Molly Malone Cook
(1 9 2 5 – 2 0 0 5)

CONTENTS

Abba Lot went to see Abba Joseph and said to him, "Abba, as far as I can I say my little office, I fast a little, I pray and meditate, I live in peace and as far as I can, I purify my thoughts. What else can I do?" Then the old man stood up and stretched his hands towards heaven. His fingers became like ten lamps of fire and he said to him, "If you will, you can become all flame."

From *The Sayings of the Desert Fathers*

THIRST

Messenger

My work is loving the world.
Here the sunflowers, there the hummingbird—
     equal seekers of sweetness.
Here the quickening yeast; there the blue plums.
Here the clam deep in the speckled sand.

Are my boots old? Is my coat torn?
Am I no longer young, and still not half-perfect? Let me
     keep my mind on what matters,
which is my work,

which is mostly standing still and learning to be
     astonished.
The phoebe, the delphinium.
The sheep in the pasture, and the pasture.
Which is mostly rejoicing, since all the ingredients are here,

which is gratitude, to be given a mind and a heart
     and these body-clothes,
a mouth with which to give shouts of joy
     to the moth and the wren, to the sleepy dug-up clam,
telling them all, over and over, how it is
     that we live forever.

Walking Home from Oak-Head

There is something
  about the snow-laden sky
    in winter
      in the late afternoon

that brings to the heart elation
  and the lovely meaninglessness
    of time.
      Whenever I get home—whenever—

somebody loves me there.
  Meanwhile
    I stand in the same dark peace
      as any pine tree,

or wander on slowly
  like the still unhurried wind,
    waiting,
      as for a gift,

for the snow to begin
  which it does
    at first casually,
      then, irrepressibly.

Wherever else I live—
  in music, in words,
    in the fires of the heart,
      I abide just as deeply

in this nameless, indivisible place,
   this world,
      which is falling apart now,
         which is white and wild,

which is faithful beyond all our expressions of faith,
   our deepest prayers.
      Don't worry, sooner or later I'll be home.
      Red-cheeked from the roused wind,

I'll stand in the doorway
   stamping my boots and slapping my hands,
      my shoulders
         covered with stars.

When I Am Among the Trees

When I am among the trees,
especially the willows and the honey locust,
equally the beech, the oaks and the pines,
they give off such hints of gladness.
I would almost say that they save me, and daily.

I am so distant from the hope of myself,
in which I have goodness, and discernment,
and never hurry through the world
    but walk slowly, and bow often.

Around me the trees stir in their leaves
and call out, "Stay awhile."
The light flows from their branches.

And they call again, "It's simple," they say,
"and you too have come
into the world to do this, to go easy, to be filled
with light, and to shine."

The Poet Visits the Museum of Fine Arts

For a long time
   I was not even
      in this world, yet
         every summer

every rose
   opened in perfect sweetness
      and lived
         in gracious repose,

in its own exotic fragrance,
   in its huge willingness to give
      something, from its small self,
         to the entirety of the world.

I think of them, thousands upon thousands,
   in many lands,
      whenever summer came to them,
         rising

out of the patience of patience,
   to leaf and bud and look up
      into the blue sky
         or, with thanks,

into the rain
   that would feed
      their thirsty roots
         latched into the earth—

sandy or hard, Vermont or Arabia,
    what did it matter,
        the answer was simply to rise
           in joyfulness, all their days.

Have I found any better teaching?
    Not ever, not yet.
        Last week I saw my first Botticelli
        and almost fainted,

and if I could I would paint like that
    but am shelved somewhere below, with a few songs
        about roses: teachers, also, of the ways
           toward thanks, and praise.

Musical Notation: 1

The physicality of the religious poets should not be taken idly. He or she, who loves God, will look most deeply into His works. Clouds are not only vapor, but shape, mobility, silky sacks of nourishing rain. The pear orchard is not only profit, but a paradise of light. The luna moth, who lives but a few days, sometimes only a few hours, has a pale green wing whose rim is like a musical notation. Have you noticed?

We had a dog once that adored flowers; no matter how briskly she went through the fields, she must stop and consider the lilies, tiger lilies, and other blossoming things along her way. Another dog of our household loved sunsets and would run off in the evenings to the most western part of the shore and sit down on his haunches for the whole show, that pink and peach colored swollenness. Then home he would come trotting in the alpenglow, that happy dog.

Ribbon Snake Asleep in the Sun

I come upon him and he is
    startled; he glides
to the rock's rim; he wheels, setting in motion
    the stripes of his body, yet not going
anywhere. And, though the books say
    it can't be done, since his eyes are set
too far apart in the narrow skull, I'm not
    lying when I say that he lifts his face and looks

into my eyes and I look back until
    we are both staring hard
at each other. He wants to know
    just where in this bright, blue-faced world
he might be safe. He wants to go on with the
    flow of his life. Then he straightens
his shining back and drops

from the rocks and rockets through
    the tangle of weeds, sliding, as he goes, over
my bare foot. Then it vanishes
    into the shade and the grass, down to
some slubby stream, having
    startled me in return. But this is a
small matter. What I would speak of, rather,
    is the weightless string of his actually soft and
nervous body; the nameless stars of its eyes.

When the Roses Speak, I Pay Attention

"As long as we are able to
be extravagant we will be
hugely and damply
extravagant. Then we will drop
foil by foil to the ground. This
is our unalterable task, and we do it
joyfully."

And they went on. "Listen,
the heart-shackles are not, as you think,
death, illness, pain,
unrequited hope, not loneliness, but

lassitude, rue, vainglory, fear, anxiety,
selfishness."

Their fragrance all the while rising
from their blind bodies, making me
spin with joy.

Great Moth Comes from His Papery Cage

Gone is the worm, that tunnel body. Gone is the mouth
   that loved leaves and tomatoes.
Gone are the innumerable feet.

He is beautiful now, and shivers into the air
as if he has always known how,
who crawled and crawled, all summer.
He has wide wings, with a flare at the bottom.
The moon excites him. The heat of the night excites him.

But, where did the dance come from?
Surely not out of a simple winter's sleep.
Surely it's more than ambition, this new architecture!
What could it be, that does it?

Let me look closer, and a long time, the next time
I see green-blooded worm crawling and curling
hot day after hot day
among the leaves and the smooth, proud tomatoes.

Swimming with Otter

I am watching otter, how he
   plays in the water, how he
      displays brave underside to the
        wave-washings, how he

breathes in descent trailing sudden
   strings of pearls that tell
      almost, but never quite, where he is
        apt to rise—how he is

gone, gone, so long I despair of him, then he
   trims, wetly, up the far shore and if he
      looks back he is surely
        laughing. I too have taken

my self into this
   summer lake, where the leaves of the trees
      almost touch, where peace comes
        in the generosity of water, and I have

reached out into the loveliness and I have
   floated on my flat back to think out
      a poem or two, not by any means fluid but,
        dear God, as you have made me, my only quickness.

Mozart, for Example

All the quick notes
Mozart didn't have time to use
before he entered the cloud-boat

are falling now from the beaks
of the finches
that have gathered from the joyous summer

into the hard winter
and, like Mozart, they speak of nothing
but light and delight,

though it is true, the heavy blades of the world
are still pounding underneath.
And this is what you can do too, maybe,

if you live simply and with a lyrical heart
in the cumbered neighborhoods or even,
as Mozart sometimes managed to, in a palace,

offering tune after tune after tune,
making some hard-hearted prince
prudent and kind, just by being happy.

Making the House Ready for the Lord

Dear Lord, I have swept and I have washed but
    still nothing is as shining as it should be
for you. Under the sink, for example, is an
    uproar of mice—it is the season of their
many children. What shall I do? And under the eaves
    and through the walls the squirrels
have gnawed their ragged entrances—but it is the season
    when they need shelter, so what shall I do? And
the raccoon limps into the kitchen and opens the cupboard
    while the dog snores, the cat hugs the pillow;
what shall I do? Beautiful is the new snow falling
    in the yard and the fox who is staring boldly
up the path, to the door. And still I believe you will
    come, Lord: you will, when I speak to the fox,
the sparrow, the lost dog, the shivering sea-goose, know
    that really I am speaking to you whenever I say,
as I do all morning and afternoon: Come in, Come in.

The Winter Wood Arrives

I think
    I could have
        built a little house
            to live in

with the single cord—
    half seasoned, half not—
        trucked into the
            driveway and

tumbled down. But, instead,
    friends came
        and together we stacked it
            for the long, cold days

that are—
    maybe the only sure thing in the world—
        coming soon.
            How to keep warm

is always a problem,
    isn't it?
        Of course, there's love.
            And there's prayer.

I don't belittle them,
    and they have warmed me,
        but differently,
            from the heart outwards.

Imagine
    what swirls of frost will cling
        to the windows, what white lawns
            I will look out on

as I rise from morning prayers,
    as I remember love, that leaves yet never leaves,
        as I go out into the yard
            and bring the wood in

with struggling steps,
    with struggling thoughts,
        bundle by bundle,
            to be burned.

After Her Death

I am trying to find the lesson
for tomorrow. Matthew something.
Which lectionary? I have not
forgotten the Way, but, a little,
the way to the Way. The trees keep whispering
peace, peace, and the birds
in the shallows are full of the
bodies of small fish and are
content. They open their wings
so easily, and fly. So. It is still
possible.

       I open the book
which the strange, difficult, beautiful church
has given me. To Matthew. Anywhere.

Percy (Four)

I went to church.
I walked on the beach
and played with Percy.

I answered the phone
and paid the bills.
I did the laundry.

I spoke her name
a hundred times.

I knelt in the dark
and said some holy words.

I went downstairs,
I watered the flowers,
I fed Percy.

Cormorants

All afternoon the sea was a muddle of birds
black and spiky,
long-necked, slippery.

Down they went
into the waters for the poor
blunt-headed silver
they live on, for a little while.

God, how did it ever come to you to
invent Time?

I dream at night
of the birds, of the beautiful, dark seas
they push through.

What I Said at Her Service

When we pray to love God *perfectly,*
surely we do not mean *only.*

(Lord, see how well I have done.)

A Note Left on the Door

There are these: the blue
skirts of the ocean walking in now, almost
to the edge of town,

and a thousand birds, in their incredible wings
which they think nothing of, crying out

that the day is long, the fish are plentiful.

And friends, being as kind as friends can be,
striving to lift the darkness.

Forgive me, Lord of honeysuckle, of trees,
of notebooks, of typewriters, of music,
that there are also these:

the lover, the singer, the poet
asleep in the shadows.

Those Days

When I think of her I think of the long summer days
  she lay in the sun, how she loved the sun, how we
    spread our blanket, and friends came, and

the dogs played, and then I would get restless and
  get up and go off to the woods
    and the fields, and the afternoon would

soften gradually and finally I would come
  home, through the long shadows, and into the house
    where she would be

my glorious welcoming, tan and hungry and ready to tell
  the hurtless gossips of the day and how I
    listened leisurely while I put

around the room flowers in jars of water—
  daisies, butter-and-eggs, and everlasting—
    until like our lives they trembled and shimmered
    everywhere.

A Pretty Song

From the complications of loving you
I think there is no end or return.
No answer, no coming out of it.

Which is the only way to love, isn't it?
This isn't a playground, this is
earth, our heaven, for a while.

Therefore I have given precedence
to all my sudden, sullen, dark moods
that hold you in the center of my world.

And I say to my body: grow thinner still.
And I say to my fingers, type me a pretty song.
And I say to my heart: rave on.

Coming to God: First Days

Lord, what shall I do that I
can't quiet myself?
Here is the bread, and
here is the cup, and
I can't quiet myself.

To enter the language of transformation!
To learn the importance of stillness,
   with one's hands folded!

When will my eyes of rejoicing turn peaceful?
When will my joyful feet grow still?
When will my heart stop its prancing
   as over the summer grass?

Lord, I would run for you, loving the miles for your sake.
I would climb the highest tree
to be that much closer.

Lord, I will learn also to kneel down
into the world of the invisible,
   the inscrutable and the everlasting.
Then I will move no more than the leaves of a tree
   on a day of no wind,
bathed in light,
like the wanderer who has come home at last
and kneels in peace, done with all unnecessary things;
every motion; even words.

The Vast Ocean Begins Just Outside
Our Church: The Eucharist

Something has happened
to the bread
and the wine.

They have been blessed.
What now?
The body leans forward

to receive the gift
from the priest's hand,
then the chalice.

They are something else now
from what they were
before this began.

I want
to see Jesus,
maybe in the clouds

or on the shore,
just walking,
beautiful man

and clearly
someone else
besides.

On the hard days
I ask myself
if I ever will.

Also there are times
my body whispers to me
that I have.

Six Recognitions of the Lord

1.
I know a lot of fancy words.
I tear them from my heart and my tongue.
Then I pray.

2.
Lord God, mercy is in your hands, pour
me a little. And tenderness too. My
need is great. Beauty walks so freely
and with such gentleness. Impatience puts
a halter on my face and I run away over
the green fields wanting your voice, your
tenderness, but having to do with only
the sweet grasses of the fields against
my body. When I first found you I was
filled with light, now the darkness grows
and it is filled with crooked things, bitter
and weak, each one bearing my name.

3.
I lounge on the grass, that's all. So
simple. Then I lie back until I am
inside the cloud that is just above me
but very high, and shaped like a fish.
Or, perhaps not. Then I enter the place
of not-thinking, not-remembering, not-
wanting. When the blue jay cries out his
riddle, in his carping voice, I return.
But I go back, the threshold is always

near. Over and back, over and back. Then
I rise. Maybe I rub my face as though I
have been asleep. But I have not been
asleep. I have been, as I say, inside
the cloud, or, perhaps, the lily floating
on the water. Then I go back to town,
to my own house, my own life, which has
now become brighter and simpler, some-
where I have never been before.

4.
Of course I have always known you
are present in the clouds, and the
black oak I especially adore, and the
wings of birds. But you are present
too in the body, listening to the body,
teaching it to live, instead of all
that touching, with disembodied joy.
We do not do this easily. We have
lived so long in the heaven of touch,
and we maintain our mutability, our
physicality, even as we begin to
apprehend the other world. Slowly we
make our appreciative response.
Slowly appreciation swells to
astonishment. And we enter the dialogue
of our lives that is beyond all under-
standing or conclusion. It is mystery.
It is love of God. It is obedience.

5.
Oh, feed me this day, Holy Spirit, with
the fragrance of the fields and the
freshness of the oceans which you have
made, and help me to hear and to hold
in all dearness those exacting and wonderful
words of our Lord Christ Jesus, saying:
Follow me.

6.
Every summer the lilies rise
    and open their white hands until they almost
cover the black waters of the pond. And I give
    thanks but it does not seem like adequate thanks,
it doesn't seem
    festive enough or constant enough, nor does the
name of the Lord or the words of thanksgiving come
    into it often enough. Everywhere I go I am
treated like royalty, which I am not. I thirst and
    am given water. My eyes thirst and I am given
the white lilies on the black water. My heart
    sings but the apparatus of singing doesn't convey
half what it feels and means. In spring there's hope,
    in fall the exquisite, necessary diminishing, in
winter I am as sleepy as any beast in its
    leafy cave, but in summer there is
everywhere the luminous sprawl of gifts,
    the hospitality of the Lord and my
inadequate answers as I row my beautiful, temporary body
    through this water-lily world.

The Beautiful, Striped Sparrow

In the afternoons,
   in the almost empty fields,
      I hum the hymns
         I used to sing

in church.
    They could not tame me,
       so they would not keep me,
          alas,

and how that feels,
   the weight of it,
      I will not tell
         any of you,

not ever.
    Still, as they promised,
       God, once he is in your heart,
         is everywhere—

so even here
   among the weeds
      and the brisk trees.
         How long does it take

to hum a hymn? Strolling
   one or two acres
      of the sweetness
        of the world,

not counting
    a lapse, now and again,
        of sheer emptiness.
           Once a deer

stood quietly at my side.
    And sometimes the wind
        has touched my cheek
           like a spirit.

Am I lonely?
    The beautiful, striped sparrow,
        serenely, on the tallest weed in his kingdom,
           also sings without words.

More Beautiful than the Honey Locust Tree
Are the Words of the Lord

1.

In the household of God, I have stumbled in recitation,
　　and in my mind I have wandered.
I have interrupted worship with discussion.
Once I extinguished the Gospel candle after all the others.

But never held the cup to my mouth lagging in gratitude.

2.

The Lord forgives many things,
so I have heard.

3.

The deer came into the field.
I saw her peaceful face and heard the shuffle of her breath.
She was sweetened by merriment and not afraid,
　　but bold to say
whose field she was crossing: spoke the tap of her foot:
"It is God's, and mine."

But only that she was born into the poem that God made, and
　　called the world.

4.

And the goldfinch too
And the black pond I named my little sister, since
   otherwise I had none.
And the muskrat, with his shy hands.
And the tiny life of the single pine needle,
   which nevertheless shines.

And the priest in her beautiful vestments,
   her hand over the chalice.

And clouds moving, over the valleys of Truro.

5.

All day I watch the sky changing from blue to blue.
For You are forever
and I am like a single day that passes.
All day I think thanks for this world,
for the rocks and the tips of the waves,
for the tupelos and the fading roses.
For the wind.
For You are forever
while I am like a single day that passes.
You are the heart of the cedars of Lebanon
   and the fir called Douglas,
the bristlecone, and the willow.

6.

It's close to hopeless,
for what I want to say the red-bird
has said already, and better, in a thousand trees.

The white bear, lifting one enormous paw, has said it better.

You cannot cross one hummock or furrow but it is
    His holy ground.

7.

I had such a longing for virtue, for company.
I wanted Christ to be as close as the cross I wear.
I wanted to read and serve, to touch the altar linen.
Instead I went back to the woods where not a single tree
    turns its face away.

Instead I prayed, oh Lord, let me be something
    useful and unpretentious.
Even the chimney swift sings.
Even the cobblestones have a task to do, and do it well.

Lord, let me be a flower, even a tare; or a sparrow.
Or the smallest bright stone in a ring worn by someone
    brave and kind, whose name I will never know.

Lord, when I sleep I feel you near.

When I wake, and you are already wiping the stars away,
I rise quickly, hoping to be like your wild child
the rose, the honey-maker the honey-vine;
a bird shouting its joy as it floats
through the gift you have given us: another day.

The Place I Want to Get Back To

is where
    in the pinewoods
        in the moments between
            the darkness

and first light
    two deer
        came walking down the hill
            and when they saw me

they said to each other, okay,
    this one is okay,
        let's see who she is
            and why she is sitting

on the ground, like that,
    so quiet, as if
        asleep, or in a dream,
            but, anyway, harmless;

and so they came
    on their slender legs
        and gazed upon me
            not unlike the way

I go out to the dunes and look
    and look and look
        into the faces of the flowers;
            and then one of them leaned forward

and nuzzled my hand, and what can my life
   bring to me that could exceed
      that brief moment?
         For twenty years

I have gone every day to the same woods,
   not waiting, exactly, just lingering.
      Such gifts, bestowed,
         can't be repeated.

If you want to talk about this
   come to visit. I live in the house
      near the corner, which I have named
         Gratitude.

Praying

It doesn't have to be
the blue iris, it could be
weeds in a vacant lot, or a few
small stones; just
pay attention, then patch

a few words together and don't try
to make them elaborate, this isn't
a contest but the doorway

into thanks, and a silence in which
another voice may speak.

Musical Notation: 2

Everything is His.
The door, the door jamb.
The wood stacked near the door.
The leaves blown upon the path
   that leads to the door.
The trees that are dropping their leaves
   the wind that is tripping them this way and that way,
the clouds that are high above them,
the stars that are sleeping now beyond the clouds

and, simply said, all the rest.

When I open the door I am so sure so sure
   all this will be there, and it is.
I look around.
I fill my arms with the firewood.
I turn and enter His house, and close His door.

News of Percy (Five)

In the morning of his days he is in the afternoon of his life.
It's some news about kidneys, those bean-shaped necessities,
   of which, of his given two, he has one working, and
      that not well.

We named him for the poet, who died young, in the blue
   waters off Italy.
Maybe we should have named him William, since Wordsworth
   almost never died.

We must laugh a little at this rich and unequal world,
   so they say, so they say.
And let them keep saying it.

Percy and I are going out now, to the beach, to join
   his friends—
the afghan, the lab, the beautiful basset.
And let me go with good cheer in his company.
For though he is young he is beloved,
   he is all but famous as he runs
across the shining beach, that faces the sea.

Doesn't Every Poet Write a Poem about Unrequited Love?

The flowers
   I wanted to bring to you,
      wild and wet
         from the pale dunes

and still smelling
   of the summer night,
      and still holding a moment or two
         of the night cricket's

humble prayer,
   would have been
      so handsome
         in your hands—

so happy—I dare to say it—
   in your hands—
      yet your smile
         would have been nowhere

and maybe you would have tossed them
   onto the ground,
      or maybe, for tenderness,
         you would have taken them

into your house
   and given them water
      and put them in a dark corner
         out of reach.

In matters of love
    of this kind
        there are things we long to do
        but must not do.

I would not want to see
    your smile diminished.
        And the flowers, anyway,
            are happy just where they are,

on the pale dunes,
    above the cricket's humble nest,
        under the blue sky
            that loves us all.

Letter to _____.

You have broken my heart.
   Just as well. Now
      I am learning to rise
         above all that, learning

the thin life, waking up
    simply to praise
       everything in this world that is
        strong and beautiful

always—the trees, the rocks,
    the fields, the news
       from heaven, the laughter
        that comes back

all the same. Just as well. Time
    to read books, rake the lawn
       in peace, sweep the floor, scour
        the faces of the pans,

anything. And I have been so
    diligent it is almost
       over, I am growing myself
        as strong as rock, as a tree

which, if I put my arms around it, does not
    lean away. It is a
       wonderful life. Comfortable.
        I read the papers. Maybe

I will go on a cruise, maybe I will
    cross the entire ocean, more than once.
        Whatever you think, I have scarcely
            thought of you. Whatever you imagine,

it never really happened. Only a few
    evenings of nonsense. *Whatever you believe—*
        dear one, dear one—
            do not believe this letter.

The Poet Thinks about the Donkey

On the outskirts of Jerusalem
the donkey waited.
Not especially brave, or filled with understanding,
he stood and waited.

How horses, turned out into the meadow,
*   leap with delight!*
How doves, released from their cages,
*   clatter away, splashed with sunlight!*

But the donkey, tied to a tree as usual, waited.
Then he let himself be led away.
Then he let the stranger mount.

Never had he seen such crowds!
And I wonder if he at all imagined what was to happen.
Still, he was what he had always been: small, dark, obedient.

I hope, finally, he felt brave.
I hope, finally, he loved the man who rode so lightly upon him,
as he lifted one dusty hoof and stepped, as he had to, forward.

Gethsemane

The grass never sleeps.
Or the roses.
Nor does the lily have a secret eye that shuts until morning.

Jesus said, wait with me. But the disciples slept.

The cricket has such splendid fringe on its feet,
and it sings, have you noticed, with its whole body,
and heaven knows if it ever sleeps.

Jesus said, wait with me. And maybe the stars did, maybe
the wind wound itself into a silver tree, and didn't move,
    maybe
the lake far away, where once he walked as on a
    blue pavement,
lay still and waited, wild awake.

Oh the dear bodies, slumped and eye-shut, that could not
keep that vigil, how they must have wept,
so utterly human, knowing this too
must be a part of the story.

The Fist

There are days
when the sun goes down
like a fist,
though of course

if you see anything
in the heavens
in this way
you had better get

your eyes checked
or, better still,
your diminished spirit.
The heavens

have no fist,
or wouldn't they have been
shaking it
for a thousand years now,

and even
longer than that,
at the dull, brutish
ways of mankind—

heaven's own
creation?
Instead: such patience!
Such willingness

to let us continue!
To hear,
little by little,
the voices—

only, so far, in
pockets of the world—
suggesting
the possibilities

of peace?
Keep looking.
Behold, how the fist opens
with invitation.

Logan International

In the city called Wait,
also known as the airport,
you might think about your life—
there is not much else to do.
For one thing,
there is too much luggage,
and you're truly lugging it—
you and, it seems, everyone.

What is it, that you need so badly?
Think about this.

Earlier, in another city,
you're on the tarmac, a lost hour.
You're going to miss your connection, and you know it,
    and you do.
You're headed for five hours of nothing.
And how long can you think about your own life?

What I did, to save myself,
was to look for children, the very young ones
who couldn't even know where they were going, or why.
Some of them were fussing, of course.
Many of them were beautifully Hispanic.

The storm was still busy outside, and snow falling
    anywhere, any time, is a wonder.
But even more wonderful, and maybe the only thing
    to put your own life in proportion,

were the babies, the little ones, hot and tired,
   but still
gurgling, chuckling, as they looked—
wherever they were going, or not yet going,
in their weary parents' arms (no!
   their lucky parents' arms)—
upon this broken world.

The Poet Comments on Yet Another
Approaching Spring

Don't flowers put on their
   prettiness each spring and
      go to it with
         everything they've got? Who

would criticize the bed of
   yellow tulips or the blue
      hyacinths?
         So put a

bracelet on your
   ankle with a
      bell on it and make a
         little music for

the earth beneath your foot, or
   wear a hat with hot-colored
      ribbons for the
         pleasure of the

leaves and the clouds, or at least
   a ring with a gleaming
      stone for your finger; yesterday
         I watched a mother choose

exquisite ear-ornaments for someone
   beloved, in the spring
      of her life; they were
         for her for sure, but also it seemed

a promise, a love-message, a commitment
to all girls, and boys too, so
beautiful and hopeful in this hard world
and young.

The Uses of Sorrow

(In my sleep I dreamed this poem)

Someone I loved once gave me
a box full of darkness.

It took me years to understand
that this, too, was a gift.

Heavy

That time
I thought I could not
go any closer to grief
without dying

I went closer,
and I did not die.
Surely God
had His hand in this,

as well as friends.
Still, I was bent,
and my laughter,
as the poet said,

was nowhere to be found.
Then said my friend Daniel
(brave even among lions),
"It's not the weight you carry

but how you carry it—
books, bricks, grief—
it's all in the way
you embrace it, balance it, carry it

when you cannot, and would not,
put it down."
So I went practicing.
Have you noticed?

Have you heard
the laughter
that comes, now and again,
out of my startled mouth?

How I linger
to admire, admire, admire
the things of this world
that are kind, and maybe

also troubled—
roses in the wind,
the sea geese on the steep waves,
a love
to which there is no reply?

On Thy Wondrous Works I Will
Meditate

(Psalm 145)

1.

All day up and down the shore the
   fine points of the waves keep on
tapping whatever is there: scatter of broken
   clams, empty jingles, old
oyster shells thick and castellated that held
   once the pale jewel of their bodies, such sweet

tongue and juice. And who do you
   think you are sauntering along
five feet up in the air, the ocean a blue fire
   around your ankles, the sun
on your face on your shoulders its golden mouth whispering
   (so it seems) *you! you! you!*

2.

Now the afternoon wind
   all frill and no apparent purpose
takes her cloud-shaped
   hand and touches every one of the
waves so that rapidly
   they stir the wings of the eiders they blur

the boats on their moorings; not even the rocks
   black and blunt interrupt the waves on their
way to the shore and one last swimmer (is it you?) rides
   their salty infoldings and outfoldings until,
peaked, their blue sides heaving, they pause; and God
   whistles them back; and you glide safely to shore.

3.

One morning
   a hundred pink and cylindrical
squid lay beached their lacy faces,
   their gnarls of dimples and ropy tentacles
limp and powerless; as I watched
   the big gulls went down upon

this sweetest trash rolling
   like the arms of babies through the
swash—in a feathered dash,
   a calligraphy of delight the beaks fell
grabbing and snapping; then was left only the
   empty beach, the birds floating back over the waves.

4.

How many mysteries have you seen in your
   lifetime? How many nets pulled
full over the boat's side, each silver body
   ready or not falling into
submission? How many roses in early summer
   uncurling above the pale sands then

falling back in unfathomable
    willingness? And what can you say? Glory
to the rose and the leaf, to the seed, to the
    silver fish. Glory to time and the wild fields,
and to joy. And to grief's shock and torpor, its near swoon.

                            5.
So it is not hard to understand
    where God's body is, it is
everywhere and everything; shore and the vast
    fields of water, the accidental and the intended
over here, over there. And I bow down
    participate and attentive

it is so dense and apparent. And all the same I am still
    unsatisfied. Standing
here, now, I am thinking
    not of His thick wrists and His blue
shoulders but, still, of Him. Where, do you suppose, is His
    pale and wonderful mind?

                            6.
I would be good—oh, I would be upright and good.
    To what purpose? To be shining not
sinful, not wringing out of the hours
    petulance, heaviness, ashes. *To what purpose?*
Hope of heaven? Not that. But to enter
    the other kingdom: grace, and imagination,

and the multiple sympathies: to be as a leaf, a rose,
    a dolphin, a wave rising

slowly then briskly out of the darkness to touch
   the limpid air, to be God's mind's
servant, loving with the body's sweet mouth—its kisses, its
words—
   everything.

7.

I know a man of such
   mildness and kindness it is trying to
change my life. He does not
   preach, teach, but simply is. It is
astonishing, for he is Christ's ambassador
   truly, by rule and act. But, more,

he is kind with the sort of kindness that shines
   out, but is resolute, not fooled. He has
eaten the dark hours and could also, I think,
   soldier for God, riding out
under the storm clouds, against the world's pride and unkindness
   with both unassailable sweetness, and consoling word.

8.

Every morning I want to kneel down on the golden
   cloth of the sand and say
some kind of musical thanks for
   the world that is happening again—another day—
from the shawl of wind coming out of the
   west to the firm green

flesh of the melon lately sliced open and
   eaten, its chill and ample body

flavored with mercy. I want
   to be worthy of—what? Glory? Yes, unimaginable glory.
O Lord of melons, of mercy, though I am
   not ready, nor worthy, I am climbing toward you.

Percy (Six)

You're like a little wild thing
that was never sent to school.
Sit, I say, and you jump up.
Come, I say, and you go galloping down the sand
to the nearest dead fish
with which you perfume your sweet neck.
It is summer.
How many summers does a little dog have?

Run, run, Percy.
This is our school.

Percy (Seven)

And now Percy is getting brazen.
Let's down the beach, baby, he says.
Let's shake it with a little barking.
Let's find dead things, and explore them,
by mouth, if possible.

Or maybe the leavings of Paul's horse (after which,
forgive me for mentioning it, he is fond of kissing).

Ah, this is the thing that comes to each of us.
The child grows up.
And, according to our own ideas, is practically asunder.

I understand it.
I struggle to celebrate.
I say, with a stiff upper lip familiar to many:

Just look at that curly-haired child now, he's his own man.

In the Storm

Some black ducks
were shrugged up
on the shore.
It was snowing

hard, from the east,
and the sea
was in disorder.
Then some sanderlings,

five inches long
with beaks like wire,
flew in,
snowflakes on their backs,

and settled
in a row
behind the ducks—
whose backs were also

covered with snow—
so close
they were all but touching,
they were all but under

the roof of the ducks' tails,
so the wind, pretty much,
blew over them.
They stayed that way, motionless,

for maybe an hour,
then the sanderlings,
each a handful of feathers,
shifted, and were blown away

out over the water
which was still raging.
But, somehow,
they came back

and again the ducks,
like a feathered hedge,
let them
crouch there, and live.

If someone you didn't know
told you this,
as I am telling you this,
would you believe it?

Belief isn't always easy.
But this much I have learned—
if not enough else—
to live with my eyes open.

I know what everyone wants
is a miracle.
This wasn't a miracle.
Unless, of course, kindness—

as now and again
some rare person has suggested—
is a miracle.
As surely it is.

The Chat

I wish
  I were
    the yellow chat
      down in the thickets

who sings all night,
  throwing
    into the air
      praises

and panhandles,
  plaints,
    in curly phrases,
      half-rhymes,

free verse too,
  with head-dipping
    and wing-wringing,
      with soft breast

rising into the air—
  meek and sleek,
    broadcasting,
      with no time out

for pillow-rest,
  everything—
    pathos,
      thanks—

oh, Lord,
    what a lesson
        you send me
            as I stand

listening
    to your rattling, swamp-loving chat
        singing
            of his simple, leafy life—

how I would like to sing to you
    all night
        in the dark
            just like that.

EPILOGUE

Thirst

Another morning and I wake with thirst for the goodness I do not have. I walk out to the pond and all the way God has given us such beautiful lessons. Oh Lord, I was never a quick scholar but sulked and hunched over my books past the hour and the bell; grant me, in your mercy, a little more time. Love for the earth and love for you are having such a long conversation in my heart. Who knows what will finally happen or where I will be sent, yet already I have given a great many things away, expecting to be told to pack nothing, except the prayers which, with this thirst, I am slowly learning.

My thanks to the following periodicals, in which some of the poems in this volume first appeared.

"Making the House Ready for the Lord"—*America*

"Great Moth Comes from His Papery Cage," "The Winter Wood Arrives"—*Appalachia*

"After Her Death," "The Place I Want to Get Back To"—*Cape Cod Voice*

"Six Recognitions of the Lord"—*Episcopal Times, Portland, Shenandoah, Best Catholic Writing of 2006*

"Ribbon Snake Asleep in the Sun"—*Five Points*

"Messenger"—*Nature and Spirituality*

"Swimming with Otter"—*Orion*

"Walking Home from Oak-Head," "A Note Left on the Door," "When the Roses Speak, I Pay Attention"—*Shenandoah*

"When I Am Among the Trees," "Praying"—*Spiritus*